30 Secrets to Success in Academic Medicine: Unwritten Rules for Advancement

ISBN-13: 978-1519142467

ISBN-10: 1519142463

Sarah Toombs Smith, PhD, ELS

For Elizabeth

Happy is the man that findeth Wisdom, and the man that getteth understanding.

For the merchandise of it is better than the merchandise of silver, and the gain thereof than fine gold.

She is more precious than rubies: and all the things thou canst desire are not to be compared unto her.

Length of days is in her right hand; and in her left hand riches and honour.

Her ways are ways of pleasantness, and all her paths are peace.

She is a tree of life to them that lay hold upon her: and happy is every one that retaineth her.

(Proverbs 3:13-18, KJV)

INTRODUCTION

I have noticed, over the years, how all the little bits of information you need to know to advance does not get written down. I thought, therefore, to bring these together in a small form that junior faculty could easily digest. I came up with the *30 Secrets* format because the average month is 30 days long (sorry, "all the rest" and February). If you read one a day, you can get through them all in a month. Select three to work on each month, and you will get through them all in a year. Together, they will give you that "edge" that will help you advance, and provide time for you to have a life also.

ᛝᚱᛥᛞ·ᛥᛞᛝᛥ

ACADEMIA

ﬠﬡﬢﬣ•ﬤﬥﬦ

1. Make a plan for success.

Nothing happens by accident. Your career is no exception. You should consider where you want to go. Where do you see yourself in 20 years?   Chair of a department? Provost of a university? Senior Researcher at the NIH?   Whatever the goal, write it down.   Commit to it.   Of course, life will have its say in the matter, but you need a goal to aim at. Pick one and, as I say, and commit to it. Now, thinking in 5 year blocks, what steps are needed to get to that goal? Maybe you want to be a department chair.

So an interim step would be division chief. What do you need to be division chief? Probably tenure (of course) and some high powered discovery, plus some special types of funding or other projects that make you stand out.

Many of these steps are pretty obvious, even if the way to achieve them is not. Publish, get funded, get promotion... whatever steps need to lead you where you want to go, figure out at least the next few steps on your path. So, while you can sketch out your goals for 20 years, 15 years, 10 years in the future, most of your career plan should focus on the next 5 years. This pretty much means "get tenure."

To get tenure, what do you need to do? Write down the accomplishments you will need. Now, organize them to find out which ones need to get done now, and which have to wait until something else occurs. (Your publication in *JAMA* or *Nature* may have to wait until you have independent funding.) Having a plan, seeing the steps you need to take in black and white, these will help you focus your attention on what is necessary. By definition, all other tasks are unnecessary.

꧁ ꧂

2. Focus on your CV.

The most important yardstick by which you will be measured in academic medicine, by far, is your Curriculum Vitae, your CV. It is the record of your activities and achievements. In general, the academic medicine CV measures 4 domains: patient care, teaching, research and service. (For academia, teaching replaces patient care. Administrative duties are more emphasized in that area.)

In all cases, however, the CV focuses on what can be measured. As a result, you should focus on actual patient care, not unbillable care; assigned teaching, not substituting for another lecturer or hallway mentoring (which can't be measured or doesn't count); research that results in peer-reviewed publications, not patient aids, book reviews or other time-wasters; and service to the university and the wider academic community, not car-pooling the scout troop.

ℭ ℜℚℒℭ•ℜℳℭ ℜ

3. Write down everything.

Because the Advancement Committee will use your CV to determine whether to advance you – or to keep you – the CV needs to have all relevant information. Every lecture you give, every committee you sit on, every product you make (poster, article, patent), they all need to be in there. Develop a system (for me, it involves special folders as I finish my work) that allows you to collect the information so you can put it in your CV periodically. You should, at this point, update your CV at least monthly. Do this for two reasons: 1) it is an onerous task, and doing it monthly makes it less painful then waiting to do it once a year; and 2) just the process of collecting this information and writing it in your CV sensitizes you to the kinds of activities you are doing. Are you writing peer-reviewed articles? Are you turning your posters into articles? Are you writing grants? Remember the first point: focus your time and attention on activities that COUNT to the Review Committee. Save the fun stuff for later.

4. Say NO to time wasters.

When you are a new MD or new PhD and starting out, you soon find that you are asked to do all kinds of things that flatter your ego but do not, in fact, advance your career. Practice saying "no" to these. They include things like departmental committees of low effect. In fact, stay off any committees except those your mentor or your department chair asked you to sit on. You may be asked to work a community event that needs medical volunteers. Politely decline. How about judging a student poster session? Sure, it's only a few hours, but the energy used in that activity is now used up. You could have spent that time working on a poster presentation for a scientific meeting. Now you can't.

I'm not exaggerating when I say you don't have time for any of these. Another "time waster" is ANY writing that is not peer-reviewed and indexed, preferably in PubMed (letters to the editor, your church newsletter, local advice columns). Work up some phrases to use when people ask you to help out. Practice saying them until they sound natural.

"I'm sorry. I just don't have time right now."

"I wish I could help but my schedule right now won't permit me."

"Maybe next year."

꧁☙❦☙꧂

5. Be selectively generous.

While you don't have time to waste, you can still be generous. However, you will have to limit your generosity. Volunteer for that softball team. Help out at the local museum. Write an article or two that won't advance your career. Sit on a committee if the work of the committee is important to you and somehow connected to your career arc. But keep this effort very small. These activities tend to multiply and people will find out that you are willing to help. As a rule of thumb, don't give away more than 5-10% of your time. (For the mathematically challenged, this is 2-4 hours a week or 8-16 hours a month.) Any more than that, and you are eating into productive time. If you can manage to stay within that very narrow limit, go ahead and help out for a person or cause that is meaningful to you. Such activities can invigorate you to be more productive when you are "on task" with your career advancement. (Saturdays count, by the way.)

CRVSLLVSL

6. Focus on time management; use every minute.

Look at your career plan and determine what is needed immediately. For example, in the next six months, I need to 1) write and submit a paper, 2) finish a poster and submit for an annual meeting, and 3) prepare three lectures for my Problems in Anatomy class. Which one needs to be done right now (this week)? Which one needs to happen next? FOCUS ON ONE THING AT A TIME. Maybe the poster has a deadline in 10 days to submit; I need to do that now. Next, I have to prepare the first

Anatomy lecture or maybe write the midterm exam. Do that. Add to your CV. Now go to the next task. Keep a list of what needs to happen in the next six months, as a reminder why you need to decline the time-wasters. For the next six months, make another list.

In terms of time management, you need to become even better at this than you were in the past. Those little 10- or 15-minute spaces when you play an online game or read something while waiting for someone else to be available – you can use those to prioritize your tasks, compose an email, or think about how to organize the Discussion section of your next paper. Don't sit idle. Also, schedule your time so you have large blocks of time (1 hour or more) for writing, and use the smaller ones for editing, filling in forms, and other onerous tasks you don't like to do. (Updating your CV, anyone?) Finally, what about those months (like in the summer) where not much is scheduled? What goals can you be advancing during that time? Maybe you have time off at Christmas. Can you start on or finish a paper that is waiting on you? Look for the little spaces in which to accomplish tasks, small and large, and take those little steps that, over time, make a big impact.

One habit that will serve you well is to raise your tolerance for drudgery. Say you have something you need to do, but don't want to (evaluate an employee, start on a paper, write a report, vacuum a room). Establish a tiny threshold that anyone can get over. Tell yourself: I will work on this for 15 minutes. That's all. Then I can [insert thing you would rather do: take a walk, watch TV, leave work]. Start on the project, knowing you only have to do it for a little while. You will find that the 15 minutes go by pretty quickly and you will have something to show for your time. This is much better than the endless rounds of alternating between putting the task off and berating yourself for not doing it. The next day, give it another 15 minutes (it's OK to keep working when the time goal is reached). Give yourself a small reward – even a trip to the water fountain – when you stop. This is how you trick yourself into being more productive. Finally, do this consistently over time. One day a week will not give you enough momentum to fatten up your CV. Because you are turning down those time wasters, you should have plenty of time for the important tasks.

CRUSH·CROW

7. Write that case report. You need publications and it is OK to start small.

We all start out with grandiose ideas about how we are going to change the world. When it comes down to actually moving ahead, we have to accept that we need to crawl before we can walk. So look around you for the easy publications, the obvious seed grants. Case reports and review articles are the kinds of products you can be putting out right now. What journal accept review articles? What activities are you doing that can lead to publications? Which are springboards to papers or grants? Start on those, and look around for more.

One way to kick-start the process is to start a journal of your ideas. Write down, every night, observations, patients, ideas that come to you as a part of your normal course of work. Eventually, you will begin to develop some paper topics. As you read articles in your area, write down ideas of areas you would like to pursue. Some of these will lead you in new directions; others will be dead ends. The more you feed into the hopper, the greater your likelihood of stumbling over an idea that will lead you to the next step.

8. Build collaborations to spread the load.

Another way to get more publications is to seek out collaborators. Many people have projects half-done, or papers they don't have the time to write, but they have the data. Use professional meetings (and departmental/faculty meetings) to get with such people and work together to identify and start working on the "low hanging fruit."

Rather than approach senior people (who are likely very busy), work with others at your level or thereabouts. Such people are likely to have ideas they want to develop but not enough time or motivation to see the project through. You can help each other in this regard.

Meeting regularly (weekly) with collaborators is a great way to make sure projects move forward. Have a task assigned for each person for each week (this week, I do the lit search; you come up with 4 potential titles for the paper and a list of journals we want to submit to). The fact that another person is depending on you will make you more likely to complete the tasks. Don't get overly ambitious (we will finish the paper in 10 days); alternatively, don't let the project drag out. Use momentum to your advantage. (At this point, you might want to go to OpenSesame and listen to my free presentation "Write Your Paper in 40 Hours.")

ᚠᚱᚢᚦ·ᚱᚢᚠᚱ

9. Reduce, reuse, recycle – turn posters into papers, papers into expertise, expertise into advancement.

Each product, each publication, is a step into your future. If you have a viable idea, work on it. If you have a poster, see if you can turn it into a paper. Write another poster, another case report. Turn the case reports into consideration of practice patterns. Use poster presentations to make new contacts which can turn into collaborators. Seek out others whose ideas excite you and come up with new projects to do together.

Sometimes these efforts will turn into long-term relationships. Sometimes they will be just "one-offs" – projects that don't lead anywhere. They might lead to some other opportunity down the road, so restrain yourself from burning bridges. Even if the project doesn't lead to new paths, your focus now is on building your CV, so every publication, every product, is a victory. Since you can't know ahead of time which will result in big returns, work on those that excite you (but don't take on too much) and follow where they lead. Slog along and soon you will have an impressive list of products.

ℰℛℴℒℱ•ℒℴℱℛℴ

10. Sharpen your strengths and acknowledge your weaknesses.

One important aspect of professional development is self-knowledge. Every person has strengths and weaknesses of personality, and in terms of your fit in the job that you do. However, each is a Double-Edged Sword. Say your strength is Tenacity. You always see a project through, no matter what. On the other hand, such people often don't know when to let go. Sometimes you have to cut your losses and move on. A tenacious person has trouble doing this. So the strength is also a weakness.

Let's say you have a habit of Procrastination. You tend to wait until the last minute to do any task set before you. In general, this is a weakness, but it has its positive side: the Law of Benign Neglect. Some issues which seem like they need your attention will actually resolve on their own. (Obviously, I am not talking about patient care. My topic is career advancement.) You can save a lot of time by not responding to issues that don't need your immediate attention. Over time, you will begin to recognize what issues can be neglected and which need prompt dispatch.

The point here is that we all have strengths. Take care that your strengths do not hobble you. All have weaknesses. Minimize these, or figure out how to turn these to your advantage. At the minimum, attention to this area will teach you that others, like you, are human and have their good and bad points. So cut them some slack.

11. Use PR to advance.

You don't need to hire a Public Relations firm to help you with your career, but you can take advantage of FREE and AVAILABLE PR to advance your career. If your university has such a department, make sure they know about your published paper. Send them a copy of the acceptance letter and write a short summary of the article in lay terms. Be available for interviews; write down the answers to questions someone might have about your area who doesn't know anything about it. Keep a record of when news items about your research are published. These stories make your university look good and may influence the Tenure Committee. These are extras that are worth your time!

12. Finish what you start.

Lack of resolve is about the worst time-waster there is. Once you have made a commitment to a project (let's call that 10 hours), follow it through to completion. Most projects will cost more (cost = time) than your original estimate. This fact should not deter you. Most will involve at least one significant delay or problem that you could not anticipate. This should not deter you. At some point in most lengthy projects, you will consider chucking it all in and selling Volkswagens for a living. Resist this temptation. Once you commit, go all in.

If the project is causing lots of problems, take a new approach, consult your advisor, take on a new collaborator. If you get really, really stuck, you might have to drop the project. This should not become a pattern. Your "drop rate" should be really low (no more than 5%). If the rate is any higher, either you are picking the wrong topics, or you need to do something radically different to push through to the end, or you really do need to sell cars. Diagnose your problem and use the Friend Rule ("If this were your friend, what would you advise them to do?").

13. NEVER re-invent the wheel (but do your own work).

Your science should be original, but you can save a lot of time by looking at models before you begin a new project. For example, if you have to write a syllabus for a course, check online for others that might exist. These can help you with topics, and give you an idea of how much material can be covered in one semester. Many grant sections have models online that you can use to help you in drafting. Look through some similar scientific posters online before you put yours together. When writing a paper, get 4 or 5 similar articles to use as models. Before you write the Methods section, read through the Methods sections of those papers (and just that one section). This "priming the pump" will get you over the hurdle of starting on your own writing.

14. Have a mentor, be a mentor.

Everyone needs a mentor. Actually, you
need a mentor of some kind for all areas of
your life. Professionally, you need one for
each skill-set you will develop for promotion
(clinical, teaching, research, service) as well
as one for advancement itself. These might
all be the same person (although it is rare to
find a mentor like this) or you may have
several. A mentor helps you clarify your
goals and focus on doing the important
tasks to get you to those goals. A mentor
can help you identify time-wasters. A good
mentor helps you distinguish ideas worth

pursuing from those that will not pan out. A great mentor encourages you and confirms your ability to do the really hard tasks. Also, they write letters.

By the same token, be prepared to take on this role as your career matures. Use your experience with mentors to become an exceptional one when your time comes.

CR&d•&&d

15. Do what your mentor tells you.

Some people have great mentors, but they feel they need to go their own way. This is foolish. An exceptional mentor (someone who has shepherded 10+ postdocs or junior faculty) knows what you need to do because of their extensive experience. Having chosen a mentor, you should do what they tell you to do and take the path they suggest. A mentor is like a guide who has been down the road before; they can see what lies ahead much better than you can. Trust your mentor to lead you along the path ahead. I am assuming, of course, that you and your mentor have agreed on the path for you to follow and the tasks you need to get there. If you and your mentor argue all the time or the relationship is not one of trust, it's time for you to look for a new mentor.

This point – do what the mentor tells you – may seem self-evident. I have seen more than once how junior people who think they know everything will reject the good advice of a seasoned mentor, sometimes to disastrous result. So, I repeat: do what your mentor tells you to do. I think the problem may be that humans tend to want to find the path of least resistance; a career in academic medicine is not one in which you will find that path. Accept that hard work and little reward lay in your near future. Next time you see your mentor, write down their instructions if you think you will not remember them, and review that list until you have committed it to memory.

16. Take leadership training if your institution values it.

Some institutions will send you to some kind of leadership camp or training. If you have the opportunity to do this, take advantage of it. Such training looks great on your resume and indicates that you are someone who intends to move up the ladder. If you have not considered yourself a leader, get advice from others before you turn down this opportunity. You might be more ready for this than you think.

17. Develop ancillary skills.

Specialization is no longer enough. You
need to know a lot more than what you got
your degree in. Work to develop other skills
that will enhance your work in some way. If
you use statistics but that is not your area,
get a degree or certificate in that. If you
need to know another specialization besides
your own, take a short course or workshop
in that area. Put those certificates on your
wall. Most people will tend to stop when
they think they "know enough." Your
commitment to new knowledge will make

you more valuable and will expand your
ability to ask research questions.

18. Accept impermanence.

Everything in life is temporary. The death rate for the human race is 100%. In your professional life, also, everything is temporary. One reason to keep your CV up-to-date is that opportunity will come your way when you are focused on something else. This position was good for you when you accepted it; another might be better for you now, or in 5 years. Stay flexible and open to opportunities that might develop. They will lead you to better things you cannot anticipate.

A sad part of this topic is that people respond to you based on first impressions. If that impression is more than 10 years old or based on your training period, those people will tend to always see you as "a junior person." It will be nearly impossible for them to re-think who you are. If the perceptions of others are holding you back, accept the possibility that you might need to move elsewhere to benefit from a more recent, more accurate first impression.

⊄ ⵛⵣ ⴷ•ⴽ ⵀⵓ ⵉ

APPEARANCE

꧁ꕥꕤ꧂

19. Look and act the part (of someone promotable).

You should dress like the professional you are. Take care not to look like a scraggly graduate student. Also, you should not look overly polished (look like a professional, not a trophy wife). Carry yourself like an adult, too. Don't flop into chairs or shuffle about. There is a reason bankers dress conservatively: their appearance is designed to instill in you a confidence that you can trust them with your money. In the same way, always look professional at work. Casual days can be observed when you are tenured. For now, always dress at least as formally as the Chair of your department. Look like a "sure bet" to the faculty who will be voting on your tenure. Since you do not know who will be on that committee, look neat all the time.

20. Take voice lessons.

Assess your speaking voice. If it is anything other than pleasant, find a voice coach and start training your voice. Most people pitch their voice too high. In either sex, this makes you sound callow and immature. It can be annoying to listen to, but no one will say anything about it. However, the unconscious effect will be felt by people, whether they know it or not.

Think of the opposite. A person with a well-modulated voice is a pleasure to listen to, whatever that person is saying. This is one attribute that makes actors so pleasant: they have trained their voices to be as clear and pleasant as possible. A voice coach can help with this and it won't take forever for you to improve your sound impression. Even if you don't need a coach, make sure your speaking voice is the best you can make it.

ATTITUDE

ఠ ಐಲ ಠ•ಲ ఠಠ ಐ

21. Strive for perfection, but accept "good enough."

It goes without being said that we all want to accomplish 100% all the time. Trying to achieve this standard, however, will actually kill you (see "karōshi," death from overwork). You have to know when to let well enough alone. Of course, most people need to learn first to work hard enough to actually finish the project (we tend to think we can accomplish tasks quicker and easier than is actually possible). There comes a point on the project when all you can do is make it worse. That is the time to stop and let go of the project. Accept that this was the best you could do with the time and effort you had to work with. Then, after taking a break, start on the next project.

22. Remember the Sabbath day, to keep it holy.

Every religion, every culture incorporates some idea of rest (or holy days, that is, "holidays"). The person who neglects time to rest and recuperate is the person on the fast track to burn out. Whether you use the Sabbath or some other system, you need regular periods of inaction, both daily and weekly. These periods help you re-charge so you have energy to keep at all the tasks before you. They also give the unconscious time to work on the intellectual problems you encounter. This is why you will leave for the day without being able to see a way through to the next step, but it comes to you when you wake up or when you start to work on it again the next day. Respect your physical limitations and don't think you can build a career on caffeine.

ᚠᚱᛟᛞᛁ•ᚱᚢᚠᚢᛋ

23. Be afraid, but do new things anyway.

Anything new is scary. When it is tied to your ability to survive, it is scarier still. That being said, fear should not keep you from trying new directions in your career. Indeed, only by trying new, scary things will you develop professionally. That being said, you should stick to fairly predictable areas for the time being (until you have a few publications under your belt). But take some time to go into uncharted waters. Treasure rarely lies where everyone scuba-dives (to extend the metaphor).

24. Trust serendipity.

Someone once said, "The harder I work, the luckier I get." What this means is that the more you do, the more opportunities seem to spring at you, the more people you can collaborate with, the more ideas you have and the more you can advance your career with minimal effort. This is one of those paradoxical laws of the universe. You can't explain it, but it works. Look for such happy accidents.

25. Embrace the drudgery because it leads to success.

Any job involves drudgery some of the time. That stack of review articles you must read can seem pretty dry, especially on a Friday afternoon (or on a Saturday afternoon). However, doing "just enough" will not get your success in academic medicine. Far from it. You must be willing to slog through a lot of tasks that are unpleasant, or even just tedious. Find a way to accept this fact of life because some things you just can't delegate (and updating your CV is only one of those). Push yourself to embrace the unappealing tasks because once they are done, you can move along to activities that are more pleasant.

26. Never give up, never surrender. Once you have set your feet on the path, pursue your goal relentlessly.

Don't second-guess yourself. Once you decide to pursue a goal (say, tenure), work toward that goal with all your effort. Many people sabotage themselves by wasting time thinking they are not good enough, second-guessing their decisions, comparing themselves to others. Once you decide on a goal – and you have thought the matter through – consider the issue settled, and focus your energy on accomplishing the task.

ᜱᜪᜮᜫ•ᜮᜪᜮᜱ

27. Don't compare yourself to others.

There will always be someone who gets there ahead of you, who is faster than you, smarter than you, who can do things more easily than you. Their story is not your story. You can't know what effort it takes for others. Making such comparisons cannot help you; they can only discourage you. Life is not a race with others; the only person you should compete with is yourself. Do your best every day, and ignore how much effort it takes others to succeed. You can't really know that, anyway.

ℰℛℰℒ𝒮•ℒ𝒮ℰℛℰ

28. Tolerate uncertainty but always have a "Plan B."

In terms of advancement, people often stay at a job because of fear of the unknown. Some unscrupulous persons take advantage of this human tendency to hang onto people without advancing them. This is wrong, but if you see the pattern in your career, you must take initiative to break the cycle.

If managers promises advancement but don't deliver, give them reasonable opportunity to make good. If they don't (say, within 2-3 years), then leave. If you stay, you are like the battered spouse who makes excuses for the person who hits them. Don't subject yourself to that.

29. Recognize that the shortest distance between two points is not always a straight line.

In life, setbacks occur to all of us. Although we like to pretend that an academic career is a rigid advance from one success to another, we will admit (in private) that, in our case, it did not proceed that way. When set-backs occur, they can be opportunities to learn something or go in a new direction. Your career is unlikely to take a straight path from the obvious to the more obvious. Rather than being an anomaly, the winding path is likely the one more travelled.

30. Act as if someone is always watching. Because someone always is.

Until you achieve that all-important tenure, you are a kind of temporary employee. These years are a kind of extended interview. Your actions will be scrutinized, your accomplishments picked over. Whether you like it or not, your position puts you in a kind of fishbowl. You should act accordingly.

❦ ❧❦❧•❦❧❦❧

30 SECRETS

1. Make a plan for success.

2. Focus on your CV.

3. Write down everything.

4. Say NO to time wasters.

5. Be selectively generous.

6. Focus on time management; use every minute.

7. Write that case report. You need publications and it is OK to start small.

8. Build collaborations to spread the load.

9. Reduce, reuse, recycle – turn posters into papers, papers into expertise, expertise into advancement.

10. Sharpen your strengths and acknowledge your weaknesses.

11. Use PR to advance.

12. Finish what you start.

13. NEVER re-invent the wheel (but do your own work).

14. Have a mentor, be a mentor.

15. Do what your mentor tells you.

16. Take leadership training if your institution values it.

17. Develop ancillary skills.

18. Accept impermanence.

19. Look and act the part (of someone promotable).

20. Take voice lessons.

21. Strive for perfection, but accept "good enough."

22. Remember the Sabbath day, to keep it holy.

23. Be afraid, but do new things anyway.

24. Trust serendipity.

25. Embrace the drudgery because it leads to success.

26. Never give up, never surrender. Once you have set your feet on the path, pursue your goal relentlessly.

27. Don't compare yourself to others.

28. Tolerate uncertainty but always have a "Plan B."

29. Recognize that the shortest distance between two points is not always a straight line.

30. Act as if someone is always watching. Because someone always is.

AFTERWORD

These secrets should set you on the path to success. While it is true that success is "1% inspiration, 99% perspiration," effort must be coupled with good habits and a knowledge of the rules of human behavior. For example, people need rest. If you don't rest your mind and body, you will eventually burn out, with tragic consequences. Be relentless, but measured. Take the steps that make sense for you and treat others as you would like to be treated. In this way, you will have no regret in your pursuit of advancement in Academic Medicine. I wish you well on your journey.

About the Author

Sarah Toombs Smith is an accomplished writer, editor, teacher and writing coach. After two decades in academic medicine, she has seen it all. In particular, she has seen how fellows and junior faculty struggle to balance the many demands of their position, often failing in crucial areas because no one told them how to achieve success. Here, for the first time, she shares the little known keys to getting ahead and making your career.